MY DAY AT THE ZOO

REPTILE PARK

Terry Jennings

Consultant: Steve Parker
Editor: Eve Marleau
Designer and
Picture Researcher: Liz Wiffen

First published in the UK in 2010 by
QED Publishing
A Quarto Group Company
226 City Road
London EC1V 2TT
www.qed-publishing.co.uk

ISBN 978 1 84835 471 5

Printed in China

The words in **bold** are explained
in the Glossary on page 22.

Contents

Reptile parks

We are going to a reptile park today. Reptiles are animals such as lizards, snakes, crocodiles, turtles and tortoises.

→ Reptiles like this lizard have scaly skin.

Reptile watch

■ CROCODILE HABITAT

ENDANGERED

The map shows where in the world the animal groups live. Information about the most rare or at-risk animals is shown under the endangered symbol.

A reptile is an animal with dry, scaly skin. Reptiles are **cold-blooded** animals, so their bodies are at the same temperature as the area that they live in. Most reptiles in the wild live in warm places on land, and most lay eggs.

The animals in reptile parks are kept in enclosures where they have space to move around. Reptile parks also breed animals that are in danger of becoming **extinct**. Reptile parks and zoos work to protect the environment these animals come from, too.

→ The snakes and many other reptiles in a reptile park are safely behind glass.

The Swallowing

← Some larger reptiles are in special **enclosures** from which they cannot escape.

5

Cobras and other snakes

ENDANGERED
PHILIPPINE
Location:
Philippines
Population:
less than 5000

Unlike most animals, snakes do not have legs. Snakes can move very quickly to catch their **prey**. They usually slither along the ground, but some kinds can climb trees as well.

One of the snakes I saw was a cobra. Cobras are **poisonous** snakes found in Africa, India and Asia. The cobra spreads out its neck to make itself look bigger and more frightening.

→ The cobra often rears up when it is ready to bite.

In another tank was a boa constrictor. Boa constrictors do not have poisonous **fangs**. Instead, they coil their body around prey and squeeze it to death.

→ This common boa can grow to be 4 metres long. It squeezes its prey to death.

↑ Snakes can shed their skin up to eight times in one year.

ZOO STARS

One reason why some reptiles face extinction is because they are taken from the wild and sold as pets. In 2009, a man was arrested at an airport in Norway. He had 14 royal pythons and 10 geckos taped to his body. He had hoped to sell them!

ENDANGERED
SIAMESE
CROCODILE
Location:
Cambodia
Population:
Less than 250

Crocodiles

Crocodiles live in rivers and lakes in hot countries. They eat anything from fish and birds to large animals such as gazelles.

Crocodiles are very large reptiles. One of the Nile crocodiles I saw was nearly six metres long. Crocodiles lie in the river with only their eyes and **nostrils** showing above the water, waiting for prey to come to the river to drink. Then they grab it in their huge **jaws**.

eye

nostril

↑ Like most crocodiles, the Nile crocodile has eyes and nostrils on top of its head, so it can see and breathe in water.

→ This Nile crocodile shows its sharp teeth as it opens its mouth to stay cool.

teeth

The female crocodile guards her eggs and looks after the babies when they hatch.

Three things
you didn't know about...
CROCODILES

1 The largest crocodile in the world is a saltwater crocodile found from India to South East Asia and Australia. It can grow to be 7 metres long and weigh one tonne.

2 Crocodiles can grasp and crush food with their teeth, but not chew it. Crocodiles have to swallow stones to help grind up the food in their stomach.

3 99 per cent of baby crocodiles are eaten by predators during the first year of life.

↑ A female crocodile lays between 16 and 80 eggs in a hole dug in the riverbank.

ALLIGATOR HABITAT

ENDANGERED

CHINESE ALLIGATOR

Location: China

Population: Less than 1000

Alligators

There are only two kinds of alligator in the world – the American alligator and the Chinese alligator.

American alligators look very similar to crocodiles. The American alligator I saw looked just like a log until it moved. When it gets dark, alligators slide into the water and spend the night hunting. They eat fish and bigger animals, such as birds.

↑ Adult American alligators are black.

→ American alligator babies have yellow stripes.

A female alligator lays up to 60 eggs in a nest made of plants and mud. She digs the nest open when she hears the babies hatching. She looks after the young alligators for up to three years.

↓ The female American alligator carries her babies to safety in her mouth.

baby about 10 days old

← The Chinese alligator is now very rare.

ZOO VIEW

Until recently, there were fewer than 150 Chinese alligators left in the wild. The Wildlife Conservation Society released Chinese alligators that had been **bred** in American zoos into the Yangtze River in China to help breeding. This stopped the Chinese alligator from becoming extinct in the wild.

ENDANGERED
KOMODO DRAGON
(A LIZARD)
Location:
Indonesia
Population:
5000

Lizards

Lizards look a bit like crocodiles, but are much smaller. Most lizards have four legs, sharp claws on their feet and a long tail.

← The frilled lizard of Australia spreads out the collar on its neck to frighten away enemies.

Lizards usually live in warm countries. They need to heat up in the sun before they can move about because they are cold-blooded. Most lizards can move very quickly. The geckos I saw were climbing up the walls of their tanks.

↑ A gecko is a lizard that has sticky pads on its toes. It can even run upside down across a ceiling.

sticky pads

↓ The Gila monster has unusual bead-shaped scales. It eats eggs, birds, mice, frogs – and other lizards!

thick skin with scales

claw

tongue

One lizard I saw was called a Gila monster. In the wild, Gila monsters live in the North American deserts. Their bright-red and black markings show that they have a poisonous bite.

ZOO VIEW

In 2008, scientists working near the mouth of the Mekong River in South East Asia discovered 18 new species of reptile. The scientists are worried that these animals may soon become extinct. This is because sea levels are rising as the Earth becomes warmer. All of these 'new' reptiles could soon be flooded out.

Chameleons

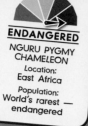

■ CHAMELEON HABITAT

ENDANGERED
NGURU PYGMY CHAMELEON
Location:
East Africa
Population:
World's rarest — endangered

The chameleon is a lizard that lives in trees. Chameleons are unusual because they can change the colour of their skin.

Chameleons change the colour of their skin when they are angry or frightened. They also change colour to match their surroundings, so that they are **camouflaged**, or hard to see. This stops them from being attacked by **predators**.

↑ The male panther chameleon can change from this colour...

↑ ...to this colour when it wants to attract a mate.

14

Chameleons generally eat insects such as flies, but larger chameleons can eat small birds and other lizards. There were some large flies in the cage of the Jackson's chameleon that I saw. When one came too close, the chameleon shot out its long tongue and caught the fly.

Three things
you didn't know about...
CHAMELEONS

1 The world's smallest chameleon is a *Brookesia* chameleon from Madagascar. It is only 3.3 centimetres long.

2 Chameleons can move each eye separately.

3 Most chameleons lay eggs. In a few kinds, the eggs hatch inside the mother's body.

↑ This Jackson's chameleon from East Africa is using its tail to hold onto a flower.

Tortoises

ENDANGERED
GALAPAGOS
TORTOISE
Location:
Galapagos Islands
Population:
9000 to 10,000

Tortoises have a hard shell covering their soft body. They live in places with a warm climate, such as South America. Tortoises can live to be more than 150 years old.

↓ Galapagos tortoises have a large, knobbly shell.

1.2 metres long

Tortoises' shells are very heavy, so these reptiles can only move slowly. The tortoise that I saw was a Galapagos tortoise. This is the world's largest **species** of tortoise. It can grow to be 1.2 metres long and weigh up to 215 kilograms.

Tortoises eat grass and other leaves, as well as fruit. They have a mouth a bit like a bird's beak, but no teeth. Instead, they cut up their food with their sharp jaws. Tortoises lay their eggs on land.

↑ The Indian starred tortoise has star–shaped markings on its knobbly shell.

★ ZOO STARS

In June 2006, Harriet the tortoise celebrated her 175th birthday at a zoo in Australia. She weighed 150 kilograms and was about the size of a dinner table. She died of old age a few months later.

↑ The desert tortoise from the southwest United States and Mexico has shovel–shaped front feet.

Turtles and terrapins

■ TURTLE AND TERRAPIN HABITAT

ENDANGERED
WESTERN SWAMP
TURTLE
Location:
Australia
Population:
130 in wild,
200 in zoos

Like tortoises, turtles and terrapins have shells.
Turtles are found in fresh water and the sea in
the warmer parts of the world, such as Asia.
Terrapins are smaller turtles that are found in
fresh water, such as lakes and rivers.

Many turtles spend nearly all of their
life in the sea. Only the female turtles
ever return to land. They crawl up
to the beach to lay their eggs. The
females bury their eggs in a hole in the
sand and then they return to the sea.

↓ The
loggerhead sea
turtle can weigh
as much as
three people!

Like turtles, terrapins lay their eggs on land. Newborn terrapins are about 2 centimetres long. Within three years, terrapins will grow to about 12 centimetres long. Terrapins can live for 70 years.

← This terrapin is laying her eggs in a hole in the sand of a beach.

★ ZOO STARS

In 2009, a group called the Animal Guardians Association took a turtle with a broken shell to a hospital for treatment in Thailand. The doctors made a pretend shell to fit over its shell. This shell will fall off when its own shell is healed.

↑ Newly hatched baby turtles face many dangers as they crawl down the beach towards the sea.

Rattlesnakes

Rattlesnakes are found in North and South America. They are named after the rattling noise they make with their tail, which warns other animals they are poisonous.

■ RATTLESNAKE HABITAT

ENDANGERED
ARUBA ISLAND RATTLESNAKE
Location:
Aruba Island, Caribbean
Population:
230

↓ The western diamondback rattlesnake opens its mouth very wide, stabbing its fangs into its victim.

fangs

There are about 30 different kinds of rattlesnake. I saw a western diamondback rattlesnake at the reptile park. Rattlesnakes find their prey by smelling with their forked tongue, not their nostrils. Rattlesnakes feed on small animals, such as mice.

At the end of the rattlesnake's tail are some hard, loose pieces of skin. They are made of the same material as your fingernails. It is this skin that produces the rattling sound when the angry or frightened snake wags its tail.

↓ This rattlesnake uses its forked tongue to smell its prey.

forked tongue

rattle

← The rattlesnake's rattle is at the tip of its tail.

ZOO VIEW

In Canada, many rattlesnakes are killed because people are afraid of being bitten by them. Toronto Zoo is teaching country people how to move rattlesnakes safely to areas where they can live undisturbed.

Glossary

Breed To produce babies.

Camouflage A way of hiding by blending into, or looking like, the surroundings.

Cold-blooded Having a body temperature that is the same as that of the surrounding air or water.

Enclosure An area with a fence or wall around it.

Endangered In danger of becoming extinct.

Extinct Not existing anymore; when every one of a kind of animal or plant has died out.

Fang A long, sharp tooth.

Jaws The lower part of the face.

Nostril One of the two openings in the nose.

Poisonous Something that contains poision, which is a substance that can cause death or illness.

Predator An animal that hunts other animals.

Prey An animal that is hunted by other animals for food.

Species A group of animals or plants that can breed together.

Index

Notes for parents and teachers

🐢 Discuss with the children why it is necessary to be quiet and not run when visiting a reptile park. Why should you not tap on the glass in the containers, and why should you not throw pebbles, coins or food at the animals.

🐢 Reptiles are cold-blooded animals that have an internal skeleton and a backbone. Because they are cold-blooded, reptiles rely on the heat of the sun to warm up their bodies so that they can be active. When the weather turns cold, they become inactive, and in areas with cold winters reptiles hibernate.

🐢 Discuss with the children what is meant by extinction and why it is that many reptiles are in danger of becoming extinct. The many causes of extinction include destruction of the animals' natural habitat and pollution, particularly of aquatic habitats. Some other reptiles are collected from the wild for sale as pets. If reptile parks and zoos are able to breed endangered reptiles, they will not be able to release these animals into the wild unless a suitable place, free from pollution and safe from persecution, can be found for them.

🐢 Introduce the children to the word 'camouflage'. Look at the book together. Which of the animals are camouflaged? Which other animals can your child think of which are camouflaged? Think particularly of animals that live in snowy areas.

🐢 Some useful websites for more information:

www.nefsc.noaa.gov/faq

www.bbc.co.uk/nature/animals

www.kids.yahoo.com/animals

www.zsl.org/education/

www.nwf.org/wildlife

www.thebigzoo.com

www.arkive.org

www.uksafari.com

www.mcsuk.org

www.panda.org

http://animal.discovery.com/reptiles/

Website information is correct at time of going to press. However, the publishers cannot accept liability for any information or links found on third-party websites.